THE VIKINGS

BY

JOHN GUY
AND DR RICHARD HALL

WHO WERE THE VIKINGS?

he word 'Viking' makes most people think of fierce, wild warriors and pirates. Vikings attacked the Christian countries of Europe from the 8th to the 11th century. Although they were pirates, they had many civilized skills. They were excellent sailors, good traders and skilled in the arts of metalwork and carpentry. They were not people from one country but came from Denmark, Norway and Sweden. This area of northern Europe is now called Scandinavia. They were not a united people, either, and wars among the three groups were common.

EXPERT NAVIGATORS

The Vikings were expert seamen. They used large, low-sided boats called longships. They were very sleek, fast vessels, powered by a central sail and oar.

WRITING

The Vikings used symbols known as runes, which were first developed by early Germanic tribes of northern Europe. Some letters were based on Roman ones; others were invented to make easy shapes for carving. Runes were also inscribed onto special stones, with pictograms, and used in religious rituals. Most Vikings could not read and write but they enjoyed storytelling, especially epic poetry and heroic sagas.

MAP OF THE VIKING WORLD

The Vikings did not usually conquer countries, but chose to settle in lands that they liked. They went to Scandinavia, western Russia, England, Scotland, Ireland, northern France, the Faroe Islands, Iceland and Greenland. They also set up a settlement in North America, at Newfoundland, for a short time.

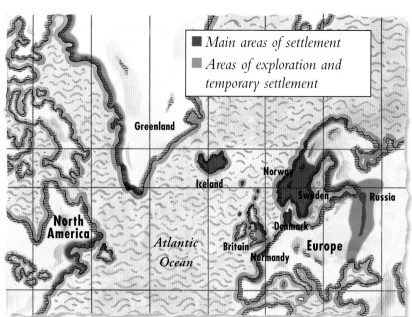

■ *Main areas of settlement*
■ *Areas of exploration and temporary settlement*

Greenland

North America

Iceland

Norway

Sweden

Russia

Denmark

Atlantic Ocean

Britain

Normandy

Europe

WARRIOR RACE

Viking warriors were amongst the fiercest (and most feared) ever known. Most of their attacks were raids, using hit-and-run tactics. Coastal towns were most at risk, as were remote and isolated monasteries such as Lindisfarne in Northumberland, which the Vikings plundered. Gradually, they set up semi-permanent bases from which to launch attacks further inland.

SIGN OF SUCCESS

This solid silver armband shows how skilled Vikings were with metal. Both men and women loved to wear jewellery, such as brooches, armbands, rings and necklaces. Wearing fine jewellery was a sign of a person's wealth.

SUPERSTITION

The Vikings worshipped many gods. These gods were given human personalities. This small bronze statuette dates from about 1000 CE and shows Frey, god of fertility.

LIFE FOR THE RICH

S ome men gained their wealth and position in society from their fathers. However, it was possible for any warrior to become rich and respected. All they had to do was to take part in raiding expeditions and steal money and treasures. The rich wore fine armour and had good weapons. Wealthy Vikings often used slaves to do the hard work in the house and on the land. The typical home of a rich Viking was a large, wooden hall where everyone lived, ate and slept. Many, who had got their wealth from foreign countries, buried their treasure in secret hiding places, because they were worried it would be stolen.

STATUS SYMBOL

This beautiful silver disc brooch from Norway would probably have been used to fasten a chieftain's cloak at the shoulder.

FINE WEAPONS

A Viking's position in society could be told by the quality of his weapons as well as by his clothes and jewellery. The pride of every Viking warrior was his sword. They were usually made of iron, with decorative inlays of silver, brass or even gold on the hilts (handles). The wealthier the warrior, the more valuable his sword.

HIDDEN TREASURE

Wealthy Vikings often collected many valuable objects, but they did not keep them on display, as we do today. Instead, they locked their valuables away inside strong wooden chests, such as this one made from oak with iron fittings. It was often the woman's responsibility to look after the chest, usually wearing the key as a sign of status.

BURIALS

Vikings believed in an afterlife and were often buried with belongings and valuables. Some wealthy Vikings were buried with their ships. A lot has been learned about Viking life from the discovery of these ships by modern archaeologists. Sometimes the ships were buried within mounds, while others were set on fire.

VIKING HALLS

Viking aristocrats and kings built large and elaborate wooden halls as living quarters, and for feasting and entertainment. Their carpenters were excellent craftsmen, who had inherited woodworking skills from their ancestors. They were capable of constructing impressive buildings, such as this 10th-century Danish hall.

ACQUIRED WEALTH

Many of the most valuable items in a wealthy Viking's house were stolen during raids to other lands. This silver cup, found in Denmark, may have come originally from a Christian monastery.

HOME COMFORTS

This reconstruction at the Jorvik Viking Centre in York shows the interior of a typical Viking Age house. There was only one main room, where the whole family lived, ate and slept. In the centre was an open fire where they cooked their food. The smoke simply seeped through the roof. Furniture would have been minimal. Cooking was mainly done in earthenware pots like the one below.

HOME FROM HOME

The Vikings used local materials to build their houses. They preferred wood but this was not always available. In the Scottish islands, such as the Shetlands and Orkneys, where there were hardly any trees, houses were built using the boulders that were scattered all over the landscape. The walls were very thick, to keep out the cold north winds, the windows were small and the roofs were thatched or turfed. Some more modern farmhouses in Shetland (above) are still built in this way.

MEASURE OF WEALTH

Viking farmers relied on grazing animals for much of their food, including sheep, cattle, pigs and even reindeer. In summer, animals might have been taken to higher pastures that could not be used during the winter. Since land could not be easily bought and sold, a man's wealth was often measured by the number of animals he had.

EVERYDAY LIFE

*V*iking society was divided into three classes: slaves, freemen and nobles, known as thralls, karls and jarls. Many of the slaves were captured in raids to foreign lands, while others became slaves because of bad debt or crime. The day-to-day work was done by slaves, and they had few rights. At the other end of the scale were nobles. Although there were only a few, they controlled large areas as 'overlords', responsible to the king. In between were freemen, including farmers, traders, craftsmen and warriors. Most people were freemen. They usually farmed their own land, but strict inheritance laws meant land was always in short supply. Land passed from father to eldest son, which meant any other sons had to look for their own land. It was this need for more land, that first drove the Vikings to seize property abroad.

FARMING LIFE

Most Vikings were full-time farmers and only part-time warriors. In Scandinavia, most of the land was either forested or mountainous, making it difficult to farm, and the growing season was short. The search for better land tempted Vikings to settle overseas.

MILITARY SERVICE

Military service took several forms in Viking society. Sometimes people helped to build camps, like the one on the right. Everyone was expected to fight for their king or local chieftain when necessary, although there was no organized army.

FOOD AND DRINK

A DELICACY

Most Vikings lived close to the coast, where there were large colonies of sea birds. They roasted the birds and gathered their eggs, which were a great delicacy. Ducks and geese were also eaten.

Most Vikings ate quite well. They mainly lived on the food they grew on family-run farms.

When crops failed or a family fell on hard times, there was plenty of wildlife to be hunted. Vikings were good hunters and killed bird, rabbits and deer. There were few differences between the diet of the rich and the poor. Everyone ate the same foods; the rich simply ate better with more variety. Meat played a large part in the Viking diet, as did fish. Vegetables, such as cabbages, beans, garlic and peas, were used to make stews. Knives were usually the only cutlery used at table. Beer made from barley was the most common drink, though the wealthy imported wine from Germany.

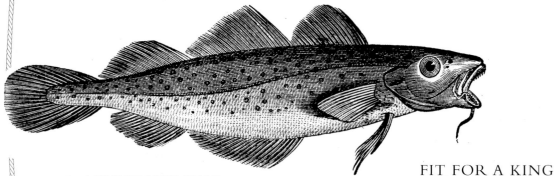

ABUNDANT SEAS

Not surprisingly for a seafaring people, fish was an important part of the Viking diet, including herring, haddock, trout and cod. Fish was available all year and was either grilled or smoked.

FIT FOR A KING

This picture shows a typical banquet scene in a noble household in the 11th century. Several courses were served in finely decorated metal dishes.

SHEPHERDS

The Vikings farmed several breeds of hardy sheep and goats that were able to cope with harsh land and the cold, northern climate. They provided a range of products, including wool (used for spinning and weaving), meat and milk.

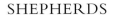

HARDY BREEDS

Vikings farmed several types of animal, including sheep, pigs, geese, deer, horses, poultry and cows. They were kept for both food and materials (such as their hides and bones). The cow shown here is a longhorn, now a rare breed. Farm animals then were much smaller than many breeds today. They were also much more hardy and able to survive harsh conditions. Cattle were also used for pulling the plough in fields. At the start of winter, when fodder was scarce, many animals were slaughtered in an annual cull. Meat was preserved by salting.

SKIN AND BONE

Deer meat (venison) was sometimes an important part of the Viking diet. Elk, red deer and reindeer all lived wild in herds, although sometimes they were farmed like sheep. The skins were used to make clothing and blankets; the bones and antlers for making tools, combs and beautiful ornaments.

PASTIMES

BOARD GAMES

Board games were very popular with Vikings, and many games of skill were based on the themes of war or capture. Favourites included the game of 'hnefetafl', in which one player used his pieces on a board to protect his king from an opponent's attacking pieces. The 'hnefi', or 'king' piece, was usually more elaborate than all the others.

*V*ikings were used to hard work, but they liked to relax, too. After work, the evenings were often spent feasting. There was a great sense of community in the Viking world, and the whole village would come to the chieftain's hall for an evening of eating, drinking and entertainment. After the meal, epic poems about Viking heroes and stories about the gods were told. Sometimes the nobles employed poets, called skalds, to amuse their guests. There would also be singing and dancing, and occasionally a wrestling match.

Tuning peg   **Bone whistle**

SONG AND DANCE

Music, dancing and singing were popular with Vikings. In ordinary households songs were sung by the family. Richer people sometimes employed professional musicians and singers to perform at special banquets. Shown here are a tuning peg from a stringed instrument; the wooden bridge of a lyre; a bone whistle; and a set of panpipes.

Bridge

Panpipes

A-FEASTING WE WILL GO

Feasts and festivals were a popular form of entertainment, and a way for the rich to display their wealth and generosity. Sometimes held in honour of the gods or for a great warrior, they were probably also held to celebrate the return of a raiding party, when the treasures were shared out.

RIDING SKILLS

Some Vikings were great horsemen. Riding a fine horse with a decorated saddle, horse-trappings and stirrups was a sign of high rank. This silver pendant of a horseman from Sweden dates from the 10th century.

HUNTING

Many of the Vikings' outdoor pursuits were a test of a warrior's bravery as well as pastimes. Hunting was popular, especially chasing dangerous animals such as bears. Warriors would often hunt on foot to show their courage.

WINTER GAMES

Many Vikings enjoyed outdoor sports, such as skiing and sledging. They also went skating on the frozen lakes and rivers using ice skates made from the foot bones of cattle or horses.

FOOTLOOSE

Shoes were made of leather, using a wooden tool called a shoe-last to help shape them. There were several common styles. Some shoes were done up with a strap and toggle, and others were slip-ons. Laces were never used on Viking shoes.

WOOLLEN CAPE

Capes were made of thick wool, often brightly coloured with vegetable dye. Sometimes they were embroidered or had fur trims.

HEADWEAR

Women wore headbands or linen bonnets; men wore woollen caps. In the winter both men and women wore fur-lined hats and gloves.

NATURAL FIBRES

Most clothes were made from wool or linen. Materials were thick and closely woven for warmth. Sometimes patterns were woven into the cloth. Common patterns were checks, similar to Scottish tartans. Sometimes pictures, such as animal heads, were included in the design.

BODY WARMTH

Clothing was often loose fitting to allow air between layers (which kept warmth in). It was held together with decorated pins, brooches and buckles.

FASHION

*V*iking clothing was usually simple, made for warmth and comfort. Vikings were not really aware of 'fashion', and they only used gold and silver jewellery as a way of showing their wealth and position in society. Jewellery was often imported by the rich. They wore many layers of clothing to keep as warm as possible. The rich and the poor dressed in the same way. The rich just used better-quality materials such as imported silks. Clothes for most Vikings were practical and were rarely decorated. Only on special occasions would wealthy Vikings wear embroidered tunics, perhaps with fur trims.

BELTING UP

Leather belts were used to hold clothes at the waist, or to support weapons. Buckles were usually moulded from metal and decorated. This belt end was made from carved bone.

BROOCHES

This richly decorated brooch (right) would probably have held together the cape of a nobleman.

UNDERWEAR

Men wore tunics with woollen leggings beneath. Linen undergarments were also worn. Women wore ankle-length linen under-dresses, often with a pinafore-style over-dress on top.

ALL DRESSED UP

Vikings from all classes liked to wear ornate buckles and brooches. The rich also liked to adorn themselves with fine jewellery, like this armband, finished off with beautiful dragon heads. This was made in Sweden in the 11th century.

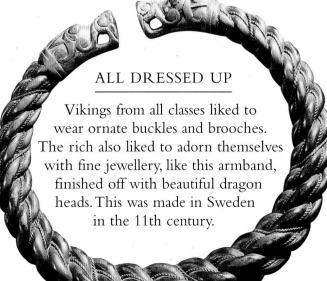

ART AND ARCHITECTURE

MEMORIAL STONES

Elaborately carved memorial stones feature strongly in Viking art. They usually tell stories of heroic deeds performed by warriors.

The Viking homelands of Denmark, Norway and Sweden were thickly forested, so it is not surprising that Vikings chose to build with timber rather than stone. Because of fire and damp, only some parts of their buildings and ornate carvings survive, but there is enough to give an idea of Vikings' carpentry skills. No wooden churches survived from the main period of Viking activity (between the 8th and 11th centuries) but many churches from the medieval period are still standing. The Vikings were also skilled metalworkers. Their best work, however, was their carved stones. They used runes and pictograms to tell religious tales, and stories from Norse mythology.

JEWELLER'S ART

This magical amulet was worn on the chest, hung round the neck on a chain, probably to ward off evil spirits. It shows how highly skilled the Vikings were at working metal into intricate shapes. However, most jewellery was made for practical purposes, such as brooches and dress pins used to hold items of clothing in place.

VIKING HALLS

Families built their own farmhouses using traditional methods, handed down over generations. Raw materials varied from place to place, but were usually timber, stone, rubble and turf, with thatched roofs. This is the reconstructed farmhouse of a wealthy Viking Age farmer from Denmark.

STAVE CHURCH

After their conversion to Christianity around 960–1000 CE, Viking kings and landowners built many wooden churches throughout Scandinavia. They built them in the same style as their halls and houses, with elaborately carved wooden staves (planks or logs) set upright in the ground.

DOMESTIC LIVING

Most ordinary people lived in small houses built with timber. As well as being easily available, timber was often warmer than stone in the cold climate. Inside, the floors were simply beaten earth, and furniture would have been minimal.

CARVING

Viking craftsmen liked to carve wood into elaborate designs, often showing heroic acts of warriors or scenes from mythology. This 12th-century example comes from a stave church in Norway, and shows complicated interlace patterns.

HEALTH AND MEDICINE

DIVINE INTERVENTION

Viking medicine was based on superstition and religious beliefs. This wood carving from a stave church shows the mythical Sigurd examining the heart of a dragon, looking for answers from the gods using magic.

The Vikings had no understanding of how the body works. They did not carry out any surgery and knew nothing of hygiene. They suffered from (and were often killed by) diseases which today could be easily cured. To avoid illness, people carried lucky charms (amulets) which they thought would protect them. If someone fell ill, there was little medical help. Natural 'cures' were sometimes tried. Vikings believed that some plants could be used to help, and some plant extracts might have been useful but others were useless.

IN THE LAP OF THE GODS

Illness was often thought of as a punishment from the gods. People would stay in good health if they pleased them. Frey, and his sister Freyja (left), were gods of fertility, love and birth. To make sure they had a healthy baby, pregnant women made offerings at their shrines.

HERBAL CURES

Most Viking medicine used the plants that were readily available from the land. Common herbal cures in general use were red clover to purify the blood, nettles to improve the circulation, eyebright to cure eye infections and willow bark to treat rheumatism brought on by the damp.

SKULL SPLITTER

Injuries suffered in battle were common and sometimes caused death. Nothing could be done to save someone who had suffered a sword blow to the head such as this (left), which has almost cut the skull in two.

HEALTHY LIFESTYLE

This face from the Viking Age has been reconstructed using computer modelling techniques. It is based on a skull dug up in York. Vikings would have looked like modern Europeans, but they had a much shorter life expectancy. Because of the dangers of childbirth women on average lived to just 35 but men frequently survived into their 50s.

THE DANGERS OF CHILDBIRTH

Birth and the year afterwards were dangerous for both the mother and the baby. Poor nutrition and disease caused many deaths, and the death rate was very high compared with today. Babies' bones are very fragile and usually dissolve in soil, but here the tiny remains of a nine-month-old child can be seen resting on its mother's hip.

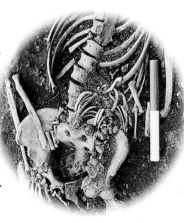

EMIGRATIONS

For many poorer Viking families, lack of land meant that the wives could not stay at home while their husbands were away on raiding expeditions. Instead, they went with their husbands, taking their belongings and children with them to set up home in the new colonies.

MARRIAGE

In Scandinavian Viking Age society the family was important in matters such as status, wealth and inheritance. Marriage was therefore a serious matter, with family reputation as important as individual attraction. The dangers of everyday life meant that both men and women were often widowed and then re-married.

HEARTH AND HOME

In Viking society, the family or kindred was very important. Any action or crime against one member of the family was, by custom, against the entire family. This custom also provided some security, because the kindred looked after a female member and her children if her husband died or was killed.

LOVE AND MARRIAGE

Although Viking women could do as they wished, most marriages were arranged between both sets of parents. The marriage ceremony was divided into two stages. First the two families would agree terms for the price of the bride. The bride's family would then hand over the agreed dowry to the groom's family. The second stage was the gift, or 'giving-away', when the bride's father gave his daughter to the groom. This was followed by a feast paid for and held in the bride's father's house.

BRYNHILD

In Viking myth, Brynhild was a beautiful Viking Valkyrie, a female warrior and messenger to Odin, god of war. Valkyries have always inspired artists.

MAINTENANCE PAYMENTS

Until Vikings converted to Christianity, women had the right to divorce their husbands whenever they chose. Often they did so because their husband did not look after them. If a husband divorced his wife he had to pay her compensation. If she left with the children she took half the husband's wealth.

WOMEN AND CHILDREN

In Viking society, women enjoyed a lot of freedom. Although men were normally heads of their households, Viking women were independent-minded and strong-willed. When their husbands were away on raiding expeditions, the women ran the farms. During these times they carried out all the duties usually done by the men. Sometimes this might include having to fight. Although it is doubtful they took part in military attacks, women did help the men defend Viking colonies. The women were even able to attend the law-making assemblies.

NEW COLONIES

Women did not always stay at home while their husbands were away. Sometimes they went with them, hoping to get land in one of the new colonies. They travelled with the men in the longships and sheltered somewhere safe until the fighting was over.

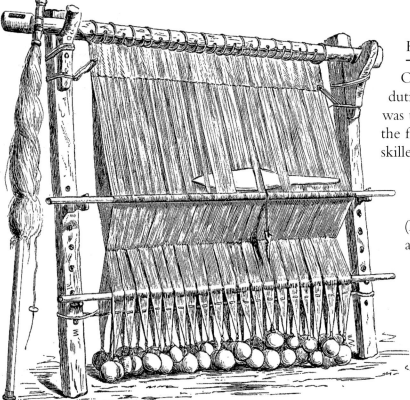

HOMESPUN

One of the main duties of Viking women was to make clothes for the family. They were skilled spinners and weavers of wool and linen. Most households had an upright hand-loom (left) which leaned against a wall. Stones were used to weigh down the threads and keep them taut while the material was woven.

A WARRIOR'S LIFE

From about the age of 12, boys began serious weapon training. Many went on raiding expeditions by the age of 16. There was no organized army, but each man owed allegiance to his chieftain and could be called to fight at any time. For young men, going on expeditions was the quickest way to get rich.

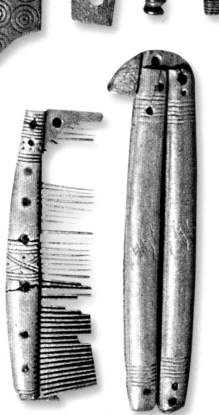

WELL-GROOMED

Viking women were proud of their appearance, especially their hair. Long hair was fashionable and women spent a great deal of time combing it. Combs were often made from antlers.

SURVIVAL OF THE FITTEST

Life in Viking society was hard. Weakness was not allowed, even in children. If a newborn baby was sickly, the father could expose it to the elements, or throw it into the sea, where it soon died.

WAR AND WEAPONRY

THE BRAVE WARRIOR

The bravery with which Vikings fought was linked to their religious beliefs. They thought that warriors killed in a battle were carried to Asgard, home of the gods. Here they fought alongside Odin, chief of the gods. Each night their injuries would heal and they would feast in the hall of Valhalla. (Viking heaven).

*A*lthough the Vikings did settle in parts of Britain, Ireland, France and Russia, they did not intend at first to conquer these lands. They were fierce pirates but they were not barbarians, and they lived in an ordered society. However, Viking warriors were feared throughout Europe for their violence. They were not afraid of death, and to die in the battle was a heroic act. If a Viking surrendered or was taken prisoner, he brought shame on his family. The Vikings' method of attack was to sail along the coast and then, during the night, enter river estuaries and creeks. They could then make surprise attacks on inland villages.

MENACING FIGUREHEADS

Vikings often carved menacing figureheads onto the bows of their ships and the front of their sledges (left) to scare their enemies as they approached or to protect themselves from evil. The figures might be mythical monsters, such as dragon heads, or carvings of fierce warriors. Sometimes they carved a god, such as Thor, as protection in battle.

WARRIOR'S HELMET

Although popular fiction usually shows Vikings wearing helmets with animal horns, they were in fact only used for ceremonial or religious occasions. The type of helmet worn by warriors was hornless. Often it had either a nose-plate or eye-guards for added protection, and sometimes a chain-mail neck guard. It was usually made from iron plates welded together.

LONGSHIPS

Remains of Viking longships have been discovered in burial mounds. Wrecks have also been found, deliberately sunk to block water channels. They were well made and of clinker construction (overlapping boards to keep the water out). They varied in length from about 18 to 27 metres, and were three to five` metres wide. They had a large keel (the backbone of a ship) and a shallow draught, meaning not much of the boat lay underwater.

FAVOURITE WEAPONS

Swords were the favourite weapon of most Viking warriors and were treated as prize possessions. It was common for a warrior to be buried with his sword, so that he could continue his battle in the afterlife. In Scandinavian mythology, swords were given magical powers and names such as 'killer'. Swords were usually single-handed but double-edged, and were made of iron. Other popular weapons were bow and arrows, and spears for both throwing and thrusting.

BATTLE-AXE

Vikings are usually shown carrying battle-axes. The axe heads were made of iron and were often highly decorated. The shafts were made of wood.

CRIME AND PUNISHMENT

PAYING THE PRICE

Crimes such as theft, assault or murder could be punished in several ways. Compensation payments from the guilty person to the victim or victim's family could be demanded, or sometimes the guilty were banished overseas. Alternatively, revenge could be taken through a blood feud, which might last for generations. Public killings, like the hanging shown on the far left of this picture stone, probably had religious meaning.

The Vikings were not a lawless race. They actually operated a form of government that involved ordinary people in the law-making process. Unusually for the time, even the wives of chieftains and freemen were allowed to give their opinions. Most crimes were punishable by compensation, but if the victim or their family refused payment of money, they had the right to take revenge on the criminal or his family. A complicated system of compensation existed for crimes ranging from theft, right through to murder. Trial by combat or by ordeal were also common, as Vikings believed the innocent would be protected by the gods. Each year at the annual assembly, the Law Speaker recited all the laws to make sure that everyone knew them.

DANEGELD

In the late 10th century the Vikings attacked England again. Sweyn, King of Denmark, brought death and disaster to many English towns. He only agreed to leave once a bribe, called Danegeld, had been paid by the English taxpayers. However, he did not keep to his word and invaded again. The English king, Ethelred the Unready, was unable to fight off the Viking invasion.

THE ALTHING

Once a year in Iceland, a national assembly met to make decisions of government. This was called the Althing. The main picture shows the meeting place, called Thingvellir – 'Parliament Plains'.

THE THING

Vikings ran a free and fair society. Local chieftains ruled over small regions, but they were controlled by an assembly, called a Thing. Here every freeman had the right to have his say on all issues, including local disputes, compensation claims, and matters of government and law.

TRAVELLING FAR AND WIDE

The Vikings travelled great distances in their search for land and treasure. Wherever possible, they went by boat. Some of their ships were quite light, and could be carried short distances overland between rivers. They travelled through most of western Russia this way. They reached as far south as the Mediterranean, and even had contacts with the Middle East. This bronze figure of the Buddha was brought to Sweden along trading routes from northern India.

YOUR CARRIAGE AWAITS

This Viking wagon is in the Oslo ship museum in Norway. It is built solidly from wood and is typical of the finest wagons used at that time. The upper carriage is heavily carved with mythical symbols.

BRIDGING THE GAP

The Vikings were great bridge builders. Their mountainous land was criss-crossed with many rivers and streams, which made transport difficult. Bridges were normally built from wood and the local population kept them in good condition.

TRANSPORT AND TECHNOLOGY

The Vikings were not only wild, fierce warriors. Mostly they were farmers and settlers. They were adventurous and enjoyed seeking out new lands. They were also highly skilled metal and woodworkers. Although they brought few new ideas and customs to the countries they invaded and settled, they were quick to pick up the ways and habits of those countries. They then included some of these practices in their own lives. The Vikings built a good network of roads (mainly in the form of tracks) and bridges. These were needed so they could travel safely over the mountainous land of the northern homelands.

CARGO BOATS

The Vikings were expert navigators and shipbuilders. The seas were uncharted so they found their way using the sun and stars and landmarks. They used two main types of boat; longships for war, and knarrs for fishing and trading. Both were open, clinker-built (with overlapping planks) and powered by a combination of oars and a central square sail. They had strong keels (the backbone of a ship) that cut through the water easily, making them incredibly seaworthy.

SLEIGH RIDE

One of the main ways of getting around the frozen landscape in winter was by sledge. The biggest were about the same size as a wagon, but with two wooden blades instead of wheels so they could travel over the snow and ice. They were sometimes decorated with ornate wood carvings, like this one (right).

RELIGION

There were many different gods in Viking religion. Many began as simple nature spirits, but the Vikings gradually developed a huge mythology around them, telling stories of heroic, warrior gods and their adventures. The three most important gods were Odin, Thor and Frey. Odin was the chief of the gods and represented war, courage and wisdom. Thor was the god of thunder, and Frey was the god of fertility. Vikings thought of their gods in the same way as they thought of themselves, fighting the powers of evil and darkness. However, they also believed that they and their gods would eventually fall in battle. It was because of this belief that Viking warriors were so fierce and brave.

OLD AND NEW

For many years after they had converted to Christianity, the Vikings continued to worship their old gods, too. This amulet, in the shape of Thor's hammer, also includes Christian symbols.

MISCHIEVOUS LOKI

Loki is a strange creature in Norse mythology, part-god and part-devil. He seems to have made mischief wherever he went and he caused the gods to quarrel. He is seen here on a forge stone with his lips sewn together, having tried to trick a dwarf blacksmith.

28

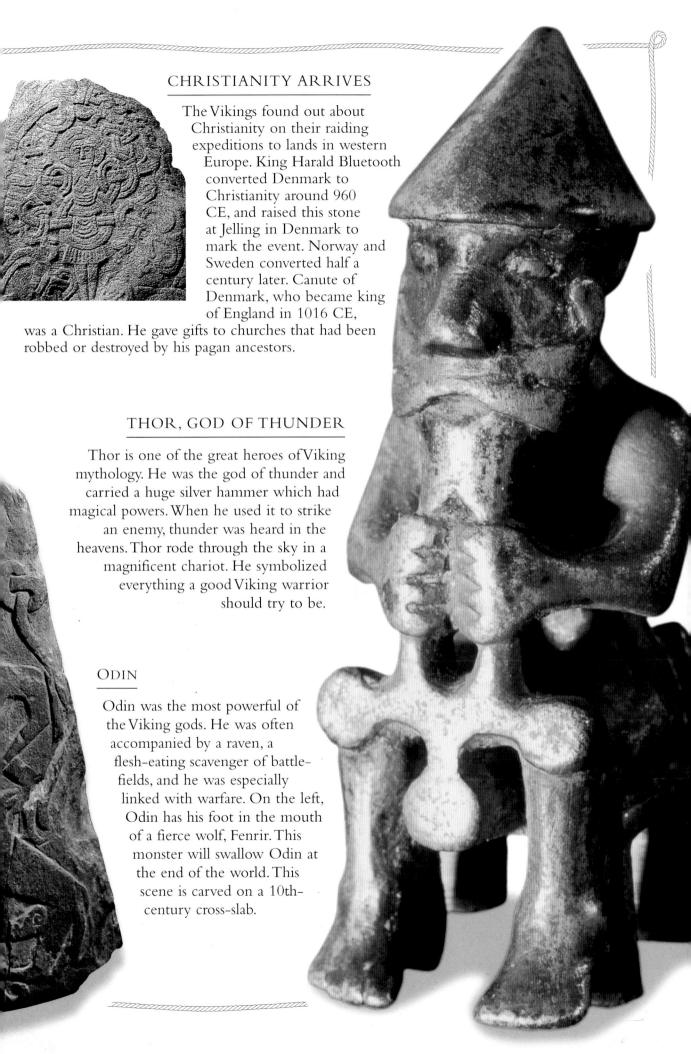

CHRISTIANITY ARRIVES

The Vikings found out about Christianity on their raiding expeditions to lands in western Europe. King Harald Bluetooth converted Denmark to Christianity around 960 CE, and raised this stone at Jelling in Denmark to mark the event. Norway and Sweden converted half a century later. Canute of Denmark, who became king of England in 1016 CE, was a Christian. He gave gifts to churches that had been robbed or destroyed by his pagan ancestors.

THOR, GOD OF THUNDER

Thor is one of the great heroes of Viking mythology. He was the god of thunder and carried a huge silver hammer which had magical powers. When he used it to strike an enemy, thunder was heard in the heavens. Thor rode through the sky in a magnificent chariot. He symbolized everything a good Viking warrior should try to be.

ODIN

Odin was the most powerful of the Viking gods. He was often accompanied by a raven, a flesh-eating scavenger of battle-fields, and he was especially linked with warfare. On the left, Odin has his foot in the mouth of a fierce wolf, Fenrir. This monster will swallow Odin at the end of the world. This scene is carved on a 10th-century cross-slab.

VIKING REMAINS

VIKING GRAVEYARD

The Viking-age cemetery at Lindhol Høje in Denmark contains almost 700 graves, many marked by triangular, oval or ship-shaped stone settings. It is one of the largest Viking cemeteries in the world, and looks like a fleet of stone ships.

The Vikings have left traces of themselves all over northern Europe, from Scandinavia to Britain. However the strongest influence of the Vikings was through the descendants of one of their colonies, the Normans, who had settled in an area of northern France known as Normandy. Centuries later, Europe suffered a further wave of invasions from the Normans. Their influence greatly affected politics and culture in most countries in medieval Europe. The greatest thing left behind by the Vikings, however, is their exciting mythology and epic poems.

DAYS OF THE WEEK

Several days of the week are named after Viking gods. Tuesday is named after Tyr, the Viking god of war (shown above with a tethered animal). Wednesday is named after Woden (or Odin), while his wife, Freya (or Frigga), gave her name to Friday. Thursday is named after the god of thunder and war, Thor.

Every year on 29th January in Lerwick, the capital of the Shetland Islands, a replica of a Viking ship is burned in the festival known as Up-Helly-Aa. The Shetland Islands, together with the Orkney Islands, belonged to Norway until 1469, and although Up-Helly-Aa and its Viking ship burning is not an ancient festival, the event is a reminder of the area's strong Viking contacts.

AMERICAN SETTLEMENTS

A Viking base-camp, where ships were repaired in about 1000 CE, was found at the north tip of Newfoundland, Canada, at L'Anse aux Meadows. This discovery shows that later stories about a land to the west of Greenland, which the Vikings called Vinland ('wineland'), were true, and the Vikings did reach North America.

THE NORMANS

In 911 CE a Norwegian prince called Rolf (or Rollo) invaded northern France with a Viking army made up mainly of Danes. The French king, Charles the Simple, offered them an area of France in return for peace. This area became known as Normandy (land of the North). Rolf and his followers soon settled and adopted many French ways, eventually forming a powerful nation in their own right. This scene from the Bayeux tapestry shows the Norman conquest of England in the 11th century.

GLOSSARY

Afterlife Life after death (in some religions).

Amulet An ornament or small piece of jewellery, thought of as a lucky charm and carried by the Vikings to protect them from illness.

Cull The selective slaughter of animals.

Feasting Drinking and eating large quantities of food, usually with others.

Fodder Food, especially dry hay or feed for cattle and other livestock.

Hardy Capable of enduring difficult conditions.

Inheritance The money, property or title received following the death of the previous holder.

Military Service Compulsory service in an army. In Viking society everyone was expected to fight for their king or chieftain.

Mythology A set of stories about the gods and heroes of a particular culture.

Pictograms A picture or symbol for a word or phrase and the first known form of writing.

Plunder Stealing goods from a place or person, using force and often violence.

Runes An ancient Germanic alphabet in the form of symbols, used and modified by the Vikings to suit carving.

Seafaring Regularly travelling by sea.

Superstition A belief, not based on reason or knowledge.

ACKNOWLEDGEMENTS

We would like to thank Allied Artists, Graham Collins, John Alston, Rosie Hankins and Elizabeth Wiggans.

Copyright © 2008 ticktock Entertainment Ltd.

First published in Great Britain by ticktock Media Ltd., Unit 2, Orchard Business Centre, North Farm Road, Tunbridge Wells, Kent, TN2 3XF, UK.

All rights reserved. No part of this publication may be reproduced, stored in a retrieval system, or transmitted in any form or by any means electronic, mechanical, photocopying, recording or otherwise, without prior written permission of the copyright owner.

A CIP catalogue record for this book is available from the British Library.

ISBN 978 1 84696 664 4

Picture research by Image Select. Printed in China.